Positive Reinforcement
Daily Declarations

Kia Amy Woods

Copyright © 2015 Kia Amy Woods

Cover & Format by Barbara Broadnax
Photography by Tasminea Woods

ISBN 978-0-9966-7030-2

ISBN 978-0-9966-7031-9 (ebook)

Dedicated to the King of my world.
My loving Father, Gykee Woods.
All that I do is to make you proud.
I LOVE YOU!

CONTENTS

ACKNOWLEDGMENTS

First and foremost, this book would have possibly never happened without my beautiful friend Takisha Johnson. You insisted I save the messages that I was sharing with you and others. I obliged, not knowing what the outcome would eventually be. Thank you for pushing me.

My dearest Jasmine Dumas, I want to thank you for your assistance with the title. The last minute adjustment was magical. I love you. Your insight is phenomenal. You are truly a woman I admire.

Keonna Freeman, my love. Thank you for generous offer to contribute financially to the release of this book. Though my pride would not allow me to accept, the offer meant more than you could ever possibly realize.

Kelli Cuff, for being attentive, providing feedback from the very beginning. Always reading each message with the eye of someone that believed I would one day publish them. Thank you!

Thank you to the many people that receive my daily messages and share how they have helped them. Thank you to those that share my words with others.

To anyone that has ever given me an idea, listened to me speak of progress and showed interest in this project. My friends and loved ones that believed in me, my talent and my artistry, Thank You from the bottom of my heart!

For those that have asked me for an affirmation or a motivational message when they were going through a tough time, your story has likely been reflected in some way, shape or form. Thank you for allowing me the opportunity to be a blessing to you and others.

I want to especially thank all my readers. If you are supporting my vision, it is important to me that you know I am blessed and humbled for the opportunity to inspire and motivate. As I speak to you, I speak to myself. I am a better person because you have encouraged greatness.

Thank you to the ones who have loved me, the ones who have hurt me and the ones in my life that fall somewhere in-between. Without you, I would not have had the emotions, strength, diligence, and foresight to realize that I can take circumstances both good and bad, and turn them into meaningful lessons.

Visit my website for ongoing updates, additional daily encouragement, poetry and more:
IAmKiaWoods.com

"More important than physical beauty, I cherish a beautiful mind, heart, soul and spirit. Without the interior to match, what is on the outside is merely decorative. I can buy decorations, but I can never buy depth, brilliance, creativity and compassion."
-Kia Amy Woods

NOTE TO THE READER

I understand that like me, you are a work in progress. Despite adversity and challenges I have faced, I constantly strive for excellence and encourage you to do the same.

We all have days where we struggle. Some days are harder than others. As someone who continues to stand against pessimism and negative thinking, I am sharing a piece of my efforts with you.

I truly hope you are able to benefit from declaring your success of the day into existence. Claim in advance characteristics and traits you aspire to or have been working on. It is my intention to provide you with a timeless body of work that allows you to begin again when the year comes to an end.

All in all, I encourage intentional excellence. Though I admire greatness of all capacities, there is something to be said about someone that deliberately chooses to be exceptional!

Most of all - Enjoy!

PREFACE

After a personal battle with canceling negative thoughts, I began writing daily affirmations. Many of my thoughts and beliefs negated what I was writing, but I continued to affirm myself daily. As time went on, I began to send these affirmations to friends and loved ones. After receiving positive feedback, I would send them to anyone who crossed my mind who I thought could use encouragement.

I truly believe that a healthy lifestyle begins with healthy mind. As I came to this conclusion and began applying it to my own life, I wanted to share my journey with those around me. From the very beginning, I received positive feedback. At times my messages stemmed conversations and/or counseling sessions of sort. I was truly humbled to learn that others were sharing my words with their other friends and loved ones.

I began saving the messages after a friend who was receiving my messages inquired about my intention. Before I knew it, I had over 50 affirmations. It was then that I decided to write one for each day of the year. I knew I wanted to publish the affirmations in hopes of reaching others outside of my inner circle.

After writing more affirmations than days of the year, I struggled with a title. It was then that the difference between an affirmation and a declaration was brought to my attention. While an affirmation suggests you are already doing something, a declaration acknowledges that even if you aren't, you will begin at the moment you claim it. With that insightful information, daily affirmations transformed into daily declarations.

JANUARY

January 1:
I leave behind anything that doesn't contribute to my peace, happiness and personal progression. I have the courage to be selective about whom and what I give my attention. My future, state of mind and quality of life all depend on my choices.

January 2:
My happiness belongs to me.
I am in control. I choose my attitude today.
I choose to see positivity at every turn.
I refuse to let negativity settle.
Today will be a good day.

January 3:
I may not have been in control of all that has happened in my life, but I am in control of my choices. Going forward, I will not be reduced by anything or anyone. I stand tall with pride knowing I am choosing wisely.

January 4:
I live my life with intent.
I live and love on purpose.
I take pleasure in finding meaning in the moment,
and I am filled with excitement about what is to come.

January 5:

The person I was yesterday introduced me to the person I am today. I look forward to meeting the person I am tomorrow. I am growing each and every day.

January 6:

I am a giver and receiver of love, strength, and inspiration. I am a conduit of love, strength and inspiration so that I may deliver to others.

January 7:

The importance of humility and gratitude does not escape me. Although my life is far from perfect, I am aware that there are people that long for things that I am fortunate to have. I am thankful each and every day.

January 8:

I set aside time for those that I love. I honor the people in my life daily. I make sure to tell those meaningful souls that they are crucial to my well being. I show the kind of love and appreciation that I would like to receive.

January 9:
Challenges are accepted and welcomed into my life. I am aware that adversity builds character. If necessary, I am willing to alter my plans while staying true to my goals. I know that I will make it through new challenges, as I have made it through others.

January 10:
I take the time to admire the beauty in the universe, in nature, and in others. As a result, I can see that beauty reflected in me. I am beautiful and have the pleasure of living amongst beautiful people and things.

January 11:
My life is constantly under construction.
I am striving to be balanced
spiritually, emotionally and physically.
I am consistently working on parts of me.
I am continuously growing.

January 12:

Compassion is a part of me.

I respond to others after first considering how my words will affect them. I release into the universe what I would like to receive.

Judgment for others has no place in my life.

I work daily to be understanding and accepting.

January 13:

Each day my experiences bestow upon me strength, courage and wisdom to become a better me.

I am an equinox within.

I am balanced in physical, mental, emotional and spiritual progress. I seek and obtain all that is necessary for my personal development as a whole.

January 14:

My words are chosen carefully.

I understand that how I speak about others says more about me than it does them.

I choose to use my words to spread joy and love, knowing that the world is in need of positivity.

January 15:
Peace is sought and treasured in my life.

I understand circumstances that interrupt my peace will present themselves, but I will choose my battles wisely. I will always seek serenity. This will allow me to draw people into my peace, instead of allowing them to pull me into their storm.

January 16:
I cancel all negative thoughts.
I stand against negative energy.
Today I choose positivity.

January 17:
Each day I do the best that I can. I use my heart, skills and resources to do what I can for others.
I can be counted on.
I am reliable.

January 18:
Resilience, courage and wisdom are not only at my access, but are part of me. I am resilient enough to face tough situations. I am courageous enough stand up against what seems impossible. I am wise enough to know which battles to fight and which ones to walk away from.

January 19:

I hold myself to a higher standard
when it comes to how I treat others.
In turn, I expect to be treated with
the same care and thoughtfulness.
I am worthy of the best from others
because that is what I offer.

January 20:

Every morning I wake up knowing I have new
opportunity, new possibilities and a chance to be greater
than the day before.

January 21:

Inspiration is all around me.
I am motivated.
I seek and receive a constant flow of creativity.
My talents are consistently cultivated.

January 22:

I have a purpose on this Earth.
I was meant to give light and life to others through
positive words and encounters. People walk away from me
feeling better than they did before. I can uplift and bring
joy through my light shining within.

January 23:
Today will have instances that may influence my attitude. I am deciding in advance that I will be positive throughout the day. I will not let any person or circumstance change my decision. I am a person of my word and I am promising to choose positivity on this day.

January 24:
I enter today with a clear mind, a calm spirit and a forgiving heart. I understand that things will happen in life that will not make sense to me. I understand that I will face disappointment. I have seen pain and faced fear. I am releasing the bad to make room for the good. I will be filled with joy, love and peace.

January 25:
When faced with a challenge, I channel my wisdom, intelligence and resources. I do not let challenges increase my stress level. There is a solution to any problem. I am aware that sometimes the solution is to adjust my mindset.

January 26:

I believe that what is meant for me cannot be kept from me and what is kept from me was not meant for me. I cancel any sense of resentment in respect to things I wanted and do not have. I am patient and willing to work for and wait for all that is meant just for me.

January 27:

I celebrate the success of others. I give the support that I am worthy of receiving. I applaud advancement and progression of those around me. I am a cheerleader for greatness. I dwell amongst the accomplished.

January 28:

I take time to appreciate the people that I love and value. There is no one in my life that feels unloved or forgotten by me. My loved ones are a priority and they are fully aware that my life would not be the same without them.

January 29:

Beauty can be found at every turn. Today I will take a moment to extract and appreciate the beauty in people, places and things. I will end my day with a new appreciation of my life and environment.

January 30:

I am an imperfect person.

I have flaws and I make mistakes.

My imperfections make me relatable.

My flaws make me humble.

My mistakes make me wise.

I am perfect in my imperfections.

January 31:

My spirit is renewed on command.

There will be times that I feel discouraged, unsure and defeated. I am able to move past these moments quickly and in a healthy manner. I understand that falling and getting up has made me significantly stronger.

FEBRUARY

February 1:
Reciprocity is key. I will never ask for something
from another that I am unwilling to deliver myself.

February 2:
Actions are more powerful than intentions.
Each day I strive to do all that I intend to do in order to
show the world the loving, nurturing, progressive talent
that lives within.

February 3:
I understand that it is important to identify things and
people that no longer serve me. I release these things and
people with the absence of bitterness. I am focused on
moving forward and toward greatness.

February 4:
I am good enough.
I am worthy.
The pain I have endured has no bearing on my self-worth.
I am and always will be good enough.

February 5:

I forgive myself for mistakes I have made.

I understand and take full responsibility for my actions at all times. I will extract the lesson from any circumstance. I am able to move forward knowing that I am better, stronger and wiser.

February 6:

There is no room for negativity in my life. Each day has room for positivity, progress and peace. I cancel out anything or anyone attempting to interrupt my joy.

February 7:

My words are chosen wisely.

I understand that I am responsible for what I speak into existence. I claim success, love, resilience, patience and compassion at every turn. By speaking these things aloud in advance, I am activating excellence within.

February 8:

I am lacking nothing in my life necessary for survival.

I work hard when there is work to be done.

When I have done all I can, I have faith.

All that is meant for me will be mine.

February 9:
Instinct is a huge part of my decision making. I trust that at the core, my instinct is divinely influenced. When I need assistance I am not afraid to seek it. When I am wrong I am not afraid to admit it. A part of my instinctual nature is to know that I am only human.

February 10:
I am grateful for my struggles.
I understand that without struggle,
I would not have stumbled across my true strength.

February 11:
I believe in myself and in my capabilities.
I am unstoppable!

February 12:
I am good enough. I am worthy.
The pain I have endured in life is no reflection of my worth as an individual.
I am in control of my progress and growth.
I am and will always be good enough!

February 13:

My energy has been restored with the rising sun.
I am grateful for not only seeing another day, but for the
chance to be active in it. I am thankful for my life as I
move through this day, aware that not everyone is as
fortunate.

February 14:

I have a heart that does not harden; a spirit that does not
break, and a touch that does not hurt. I am loving, gentle
and kind, as I want to be loved and treated like the
invaluable prize that I am.

February 15:

I am speaking success of the day into existence. Today will
be one filled with productivity. Life has prepared me for
any hardship that may present itself today.

February 16:

Life is a mission. I am igniting the fire that demands that I
live, love and walk with purpose.
I am at my best and I am giving it my all.

February 17:

I am not the product of any of the unfortunate events in my life. Instead, I have made the choice to allow the lessons to shape me. I have decided to let love bind the wounds.

February 18:

I release all that blocks me from believing in my greatness.

February 19:

I will always have the strength
to rise above negativity and distractions.

February 20:

Life has thrown curveballs.
Things have happened that I did not expect.
I've been forced to face fear and endure pain.
Still, my heart remains kind and my spirit remains brave.
I am a survivor.

February 21:

Today I will take the opportunity to refuel my soul.
I will enjoy the love I have around me and be thankful.

February 22:

I am grateful to see another day.

Yesterday is over.

To rise and begin again is a humbling blessing.

February 23:

Living life to the fullest is my ultimate goal.

I do not merely exist.

I am grabbing onto all this world has to offer and
appreciating the beauty of opportunities I have been given.

February 24:

Lessons are learned from each mistake I've made.

Every shortcoming has taught me that with time,
excellence is attainable. I am better because I proceed with
acquired wisdom that only experience can grant.

February 25:

I am aware that I attract what I reflect.

Today I am vowing to reflect peace, love, light and
happiness, from the depth of my soul to the twinkle in my
eyes. I am inviting greatness by aspiring to be great from
the inside out.

February 26:

I understand that patience is a virtue.

I know that greatness cannot be rushed.

I make sound decisions and continuously strive for progress in all areas of my life.

I never forget however, that I am living out a predetermined plan.

I wait patiently for blessings as I put my best foot forward.

February 27:

I am worthy of greatness because that is what I have to offer. I will never settle because I should never have to. I give 100% effort of anything I put my mind to, and therefore my results and my rewards should be no less than the best.

February 28:

Today will be a beautiful day.

Yesterday has ended and tomorrow has not been promised. I will take the time to enjoy today and recognize the blessing it is simply to exist on this day.

*February 29:

As I recognize that this day comes only every four years,
I acknowledge those who were not as fortunate as I to live
to see this day.

I am draped in gratitude.

---

* Leap Year

MARCH

March 1:

I am fortunate to have the ability to step outside of myself and see my life, my traits and my habits the way they are viewed by the mass majority. I am able to take personal inventory and discover where I have room to improve — even if the improvement is needed on what may not initially seem to be a problem for me. There is always room for growth and I am thankful for not only how far I've come, but for all that I have left to conquer.

March 2:

I am thankful for the possibilities this new day brings me. I am anticipating being great on this day. Joy is contagious and I will therefore help others see the potential of the day. My spirits are high and my impact is strong.
I make a difference.

March 3:

Opportunities exist all around me. I have the power to improve my overall happiness by taking advantage of resources I am exposed to and/or by seeking out new ones. I am able-bodied and strong willed. No task is too great when it pertains to my peace of mind. It is always the right time to take a step in the right direction.

March 4:

I am a student of life.

I never pass up the opportunity to learn something new.
I am grateful and receptive to new information and the
expansion of my mind. Knowledge is power.
I am knowledgeable and therefore I am powerful.

March 5:

I value the lives of others.

There are people in my life worthy of every ounce of love
I have to offer. I make time for those who make time for
me. The people I love know that I love them not only
because of words I have spoken, but also because of the
message delivered by my actions.

March 6:

I am a giver of the support that I receive and deliver the
consistency that I expect from those around me. I do not
allow myself to be used by anyone who does not have my
best intentions in mind. I use wisdom and discernment
when it comes to selecting those people that are close to
me. I give and so I shall receive.

March 7:

Despite my best efforts and judgments, I am wrong at times. When this happens, I am not too prideful to apologize to those I may have affected. I am capable of humbling myself and I am capable of forgiving myself. Additionally, I know that just as I have been wrong, others will be too. I am capable of forgiveness and appreciate humility offered by others.

March 8:

There will not always be perfect days, but there is joy waiting to be discovered in every day. I am able to see the beauty in people, places and things. I live my life with my eyes and my heart wide open.

Great energy flows to and from me freely. Each day is a new opportunity to appreciate being alive.

March 9:

Love is a part of me.

Pain I've endured at the hands of others has not blocked my ability to love. I love others as I want to be loved and I accept, as I would like to be accepted. I steer clear of judgment because I do not want to be judged. I know that what I expect is what I am obligated to reflect.

March 10:

I recognize the power of gratitude.

I understand that although I may not have all of the things that I want, things that are taken for granted can be taken away in an instant. I trust that all that is meant for me will be provided to me. I have faith in timing. As I wait, I work and remain grateful every step of the way for the strength to keep pushing forward.

March 11:

There are choices to make at every turn.

I listen to my instinct while also applying logic and channeling wisdom. I am deliberate rather than impulsive. When there is a time I realize I could have made a better choice, I am sure to store the lesson for future reference. By acknowledging that I'll never lose the right to choose, I am beckoning prosperity.

March 12:

Positive energy is contagious.

I receive the positive vibes around me. I use my acquired energy to block negativity. I am eager to pass on positivity as I have encounters with others.

I make connections with people that are pleasant, genuine, memorable and unique in their own way. As I go through my day, I vow to leave behind a trail of positive energy that others are able to thrive on.

March 13:

I am worthy of greatness. I am capable of being great.

No one is able to convince me otherwise or treat me like I am less than a prize.

March 14:

When light from within shines brightly; there will be times when it shines into the eyes of others. My growth will not be stunted nor will my voice be silenced.

My inner light cannot be dimmed. It reflects far and wide and does so unapologetically.

March 15:

I understand that what happened yesterday has helped to shape who I am today.

With this understanding, I am determined to retrieve the very best that each experience has to offer. From the unfortunate events of the past, I have extracted strength and wisdom. From the joyful times, I have extracted humility and gratitude. Thanks to both the good and bad times, I've walked away armed with exactly what I need for progression.

March 16:

I aspire to the highest forms of achievement in all I do.

March 17:

I am good at many things. I am better at others.

Whether natural talent or something I have to work for, I do my very best.

There is no room for mediocrity in my life. I'll go to bed satisfied knowing that I've put my best foot forward today.

March 18:

I understand that without true love for myself, it is impossible to fully love another. Self-love and self-worth are blueprints for what I am able to offer the world.

March 19:

There are people who have hurt or left me. Though sad and confused in the moment, I know that I am truly better off without the presence of anyone that doesn't serve me well. I am thankful for what once seemed like misfortune, as I realize it was only a blessing in disguise. I feel protected from harm and prepared for the best years, memories and people of my life. I now understand "losing" someone or something, may not be a loss at all. The universe sometimes makes room in your life for what will be your biggest win!

March 20:

There is nothing that I cannot do if I put my mind to it. I believe in myself even when others doubt me.

March 21:

There is a beautiful, loving and powerful energy that flows through me. Each day I make the decision to pass along the gift of positivity and to leave a lasting impression on the souls who I encounter.

March 22:

I embrace the many phases life has to offer.

Through the journey of life, I have continuously evolved.
The past looks differently than the present just as
tomorrow is brand new.

I understand that change is inevitable. I am excited about
growth to come. There are many seasons of our lives and
I have the strength and courage to adapt to all of them.

March 23:

I have been hurt.

I have stared fear in the face.

I have been torn and I have been broken.

I have scars that serve as evidence that I fought and
survived. I vow to turn all my wounds into wisdom.

March 24:

I have learned that I want to never stop learning.

I am a student of life.

The world is my classroom and life is my teacher.

March 25:
It is natural for me to want to take care of others. I am a one-person support system when I need to be. I take the time to take care of myself so that I can be at my best. I know that my love for others should not come before self-preservation. Taking care of me, means that I am doing a favor to those who depend on me.

March 26:
Today is a brand new day. Any negativity of yesterday has been cancelled out. Today I am choosing my attitude very carefully. I will check in with myself periodically and make adjustments as needed. Happiness is mine for the taking. No one or nothing can bring me down without my permission. Anyone intending to do so will promptly be denied access!

March 27:
Life is sometimes fast-paced.
We often get so busy that we forget to take the time to meditate, reflect and appreciate the moment. I am vowing to slow down when I feel life passing me by. I promise to meditate on words that motivate me, reflect on my behavior and decisions, and appreciate all of my blessings.

March 28:

I will not be held captive by regret.

Life has taught me many things that I will value for the rest of my days. I move on knowing there is a purpose in my pain and that if I extract the lesson, I have not suffered in vain.

March 29:

Love flows through me freely.

I am able to love without reservation and hesitation. At times, I have to love from a distance. When that decision is made, it isn't because my heart is hardened, but because I am protecting my river of love from pollution.

March 30:

Confidence dwells within me.

It is stronger than my insecurities, and more solid than my doubts. I know that I am working continuously to be all that I am meant to be. Though undoubtedly a work in progress, the person I see in the mirror is phenomenal just by aspiring to greatness. I am on my way!

March 31:

Blessings are all around me.

I may not have all that I want, but I am grateful to have all that I need. I am happy to celebrate the success of others, knowing that I am successful in my own right.

I do not envy what others have.

Instead, I focus on the great things in my life and work toward goals that will land me in the place meant especially for me.

APRIL

April 1:

Today I will have no complaints.

I will not speak ill of others, nor will I put myself down. I will dedicate time to simply say thank you for waking up this morning, for the food I will consume, for the clothing I will wear and for air that I will breathe all day. I will check on the people I love today. I will remember that their lives are important to me, and one more reason to make this a day of gratitude.

April 2:

I am encouraged.

I speak victory into my life. It only takes one life changing moment to place me in a space of greatness beyond my own imagination. I will ensure I have an attitude that is prepared and deserving to receive the blessings in store.

April 3:

I surround myself with people that lift me higher.

April 4:

I am invested in sharing my strengths and my talent.

I understand that a gift is truly not a gift until it is given.

April 5:

My energy is magnetic.

I draw in those with similar vision of peace, knowledge and understanding. I patiently wait for meaningful connections to be made with beautiful beings. I embrace and cherish relationships approved by the universe.

April 6:

I have the ability to soar beyond my imaginary limitations. Only I have the ability to hinder myself. My journey cannot be defined by anyone's standards or beliefs. I will not be controlled by fear. It is my mission to disprove all doubt that lives within. I will keep climbing until I have reached the high that is predestined for me.

April 7:

Paths will cross and paths will split.

When someone exits my life, I will not mourn the will of the universe. I understand that I was whole before them and that I will be whole again.

April 8:

I am patient with others and I am patient with myself.
I understand that we are all human beings made up of
flawed pieces of perfection. My expectations are that the
people around me try their best, and I vow to do the same.
When a mistake is made, I am able to ask for forgiveness
and I am able to grant forgiveness as well.

April 9:

I have the power and strength to release what no longer
serves me. Anything that does not add to my purpose,
foster growth or keep me whole shall be kept at a distance.

April 10:

I am grateful for life.
I've seen my share of ups and downs, but the good times
outweigh the bad by far.
I approach this new day with excitement.

April 11:

The power to choose means that I am in control.
I am able to choose my attitude. I work hard to see the
good in people. I can see the bright side of every situation.
I am making the choice to extract the lesson when things
happen that bring my spirits down. Therefore, I am
choosing positivity even at my lowest moments.

April 12:

The word "if" will be removed from my vocabulary.

In regard to goal setting, I am interested only in "when" I will achieve them.

April 13:

I am strong. I am powerful. I am resilient.

My spirit is renewed on command.

Positivity is channeled at my will.

All tools needed for success of the day are stored within.

April 14:

Today will be a good day.

I will recognize new opportunities as they present themselves. Negativity and conflict will not be acknowledged. The tone has been set. Positive vibrations have been released.

April 15:

The celebration of life will be my focus today.

I celebrate my own life and lives of my loved ones.

My soul is comforted knowing that they have also lived to see a new day. Just as I want to be loved and appreciated as I dwell on earth, I will ensure I show my love and appreciation for these precious lives while they are here.

Tonight I will rest easy knowing that meaningful relationships have been nurtured.

April 16:

Just as sun rises and gives the day meaning, I rise this morning ensured that my life is meaningful.

I have a purpose and I am dedicated to living it.

April 17:

I have the courage to re-evaluate and reconstruct pieces of my life.

What once belonged in my life, may not any longer.

I accept that.

I will not hold on to what should not be mine or what never was.

April 18:

Energy will leave my soul and attach to the souls of others in every encounter I have today. I will ensure that it is positive energy. Be it casual conversation, physical contact or a meeting of the minds, my imprint will be memorable. My remarkable legacy is being written.

April 19:

I am encouraged. I am more than a conqueror. I cancel out all doubt. As it is believed, it will come to be. I speak victory into existence on this day and the ones to come.

April 20:

I am beautiful. I am heroic in my own right. I am a leader, a humanitarian, and a motivator. I give freely and so, I shall receive in abundance. I am a blessing to others and therefore, I am blessed.

April 21:

My time is precious.

My energy is reserved for the deserving. Every moment that passes is a moment I will never live again.

Today I vow to choose my battles wisely.

I am dedicated to directing my attention to what and who really matters in my life.

April 22:

I summon all that I need today.

I will attract the energy and mindset to be at peace on this day. I call for strength and resilience as needed. I ask to be filled with joy so magical it works through me and is passed on to others. I hope for awareness that allows me to identify each and every blessing, even while they are in the making.

April 23:

Greatness dwells within me and is applied to everything that I do. I choose the right way, even when it's not the easy way. Those who know me would testify that I am an exceptional person. I stand tall and proud at the end of each day knowing that I've done my very best.

April 24:

I have the strength to let go of what and who no longer serves me. If it isn't conducive to my continuous progression, it shall be cancelled out.

April 25:

I am a protector of my loved ones. Though I am unable to protect them from all they will see in this world, my presence in their lives means they will hurt a little less, smile a little more and never feel alone. I forgive myself for any time I've fallen short in the past. I move forward today with a brand new shield of love.

April 26:

When decisions are difficult and roads are unclear, when I am fighting battles both internal and external, when I am uncertain, I follow peace.

April 27:

I am thankful for each night that has turned into a new morning, each friend that has turned into a new family member, and each dream that has turned into reality. I am grateful for all that I have today Everything that I need has been provided. I will not take this day for granted. I live and love in appreciation.

April 28:

I will not be weighed down.

I am light.

I am free.

I am at peace.

April 29:

I am in need of no outside validation.

I am able to reward myself for a job well done. I will take the time to treat myself because I know I deserve it.

I am more than worthy.

April 30:

I am strong, I am powerful, and I am resilient. I will not be broken. As wounds heal, the scars left behind are a reminder that I have survived.

MAY

May 1:

The ability to forgive keeps away resentment. I am not interested in the contamination of my heart, mind and spirit. I understand that periodic cleanses are necessary. My first step is to rid my life of toxic people and things. Second, I will forgive and be free of any additional harm caused by holding a grudge. I am wise enough to know that one step without the other will not suffice.

May 2:

Every person that we cross paths with has been put in our lives for a reason. They are either a blessing or a lesson. I have learned to distinguish between the two. I vow to be a blessing to as many as possible. Any lesson learned from an encounter with me will be a great one.

May 3:

Though we are unable to predict all of the events in our lives, we are able to control our attitude and reactions. When this world throws me a curve ball that knocks me off balance, I vow to become better instead of bitter. It's my choice and today I choose strength!

May 4:

I will not be held back by limitations set by others. Most importantly, I shall not be restrained by limitations set in my own mind. Self-doubt is the most powerful and therefore an extreme injustice to my talent. I deserve to shine, and I will do so unapologetically.

May 5:

I understand that love will always be superior to hatred, knowledge is more valuable than ignorance, and joy will always be a relief from pain. When the world needs it most, I'll intentionally be a vessel of love. I am making the decision to make a difference.

May 6:

It is my responsibility and full intention to protect what is important to me. My peace, love, hope, faith, and joy will not be exposed or trusted in the hands of others. I am vigilant and selective with whom I allow close to me. This way, I can be sure that my values are not compromised.

May 7:

I vow to be the example of the energy and people I want to attract. I will therefore never accept less than I deserve. My heart and mind is at peace because I know that by giving the best of me, I'll truly earn what is meant for me.

May 8:

I am strong enough to admit that I cannot do it alone.
I need the love, support and occasional motivation from
those around me.
In order to ensure I am receiving the proper nourishment,
I am selective with whom I allow in. Most importantly, all
that I expect from others is reciprocated.

May 9:

I understand that without true love for myself, it is
impossible to fully love another. Self-love and self-worth
are blueprints for what I am able to offer the world.

May 10:

All that I am depends on what I decide to receive and
believe. What penetrates my mind has the ability to
penetrate my soul. I am therefore careful of what I expose
myself to. I seek knowledge continuously. I shall not be
suppressed by ignorance.

May 11:

May my energy attract only that of the best.

May my heart accept that it has loved people that did not appreciate or return that love. May my life be filled from this point forward with only those deserving of my efforts, as they are always top notch. May my future be filled with happiness, forgiveness and prosperity.

May 12:

Setting and working toward goals means that there will always be continuous progression.

I will focus on results instead of excuses.

May 13:

I am beckoning the power of positivity today.

I call on healing agents for the sick, guidance for the lost, hope for the hopeless, and peace for the restless.

May today bring upon a breakthrough for all in need.

May 14:

I aim to keep an open mind and heart.

I am receptive to feedback when

I am being closed-minded and resistant to change.

May 15:
I am a winner by design.
I will fall down at times,
but in the end I will prevail.
I will always find a way to succeed.

May 16:
This will be a day of productivity.
I will be strong in my pursuit of every goal that I set
whether personal or professional. When the sun sets I will
allow my mind to rest, knowing I did my very best.

May 17:
I call for wisdom, discernment, patience and humility
when it comes to decisions, actions and encounters today.
By channeling these strengths, I will produce the very best
outcome. I cancel out pride, negativity and anything
standing in the way of my peace of mind.
I will begin today with a loving heart and rest tonight with
a calm spirit.

May 18:
I woke up today with a purpose. I have an obligation to
fulfill and a divine right to be fulfilled.

May 19:

I possess the determination and discipline to finish what I begin. I work hard to see things to completion.

"Quitting" is not in my vocabulary and failing has NEVER been an option.

May 20:

My life is guided by faith, not by fear.

Progress will require me to take chances.

I have the courage to travel the path meant for me.

May 21:

There is an abundance of love and beauty around me.

All that I need is accessible. I have the power to reject anything that is not an addition to my overall happiness.

I have the courage to choose greatness.

May 22:

I am choosing to be happy today. Anything and anyone standing in the way of that will succumb to my persistent positivity. It is my decision and my right. I am in control.

May 23:

I will not be afraid to dream.

May 24:

Everything I want to be already lives within.

I can access the very best parts of me upon demand.

I am able to achieve the goals that I set because I am disciplined and walking in excellence.

May 25:

There is nothing and no one able to deter me from the greatness I am capable of. I have proven that I am able to navigate around any road blocks, dodge all curveballs and see through the fog of unfavorable conditions.

I am victorious.

May 26:

I appreciate the beautiful things in life. The unique talent offered by others and the wonderful things provided by nature remind me that living is a gift. I strive to bring additional beauty to the world with my own excellence.

I am excited to pass on the gifts I have received.

May 27:

I am not defined by my past. I am prepared by it.

Every lesson learned makes me the person I am today.

I have a lot to offer due to my experiences.

I am better because of my past and therefore I am not bitter but grateful.

May 28:

I am no stranger to hard work. I know that my journey to success requires me to do more than the minimum.

To be "good enough" is not acceptable. I am capable of greatness and strive to produce excellence at every turn.

May 29:

There is no lesson that cannot be learned through experience by an open mind. I approach every situation knowing that I have so much to learn.

I aspire to increase my knowledge and wisdom daily.

May 30:

Imperfection is a commonality amongst individuals. Though I hold myself and others accountable for their words and actions, I understand mistakes will be made. I am able to forgive and move forward without allowing disappointment to penetrate so deeply that it becomes a crippling grudge.

May 31:

There is honor in ensuring I approach matters with tact. Even when I am angry or have been wronged, I am sure to not let people or things cause me to behave in a manner in which I may regret. I am careful with my words and actions knowing that I am living my legacy and want to leave behind one I am proud of.

JUNE

June 1:

I am able to filter out negativity and focus only on what will make a powerful impact in my life.

June 2:

I will not accept less than I deserve.

I am worthy of greatness.

June 3:

There are beautiful and exciting things in my life.

Opportunities are all around me.

There is excellence in store for me.

I am patient enough to wait for my future.

June 4:

My path is mine and mine alone.

Nothing that is meant for me can be kept from me.

All that I am and will be has been decided. I will live each day knowing that I am exactly where I am supposed to be.

June 5:

Success requires hard work, perseverance and discipline.

I am not afraid to give my dreams all that I have.

My destiny is depending on me.

June 6:

Learning is a result of living life with an open mind.
With each lesson, I become a better person.
As an informed individual, I am constantly elevating.
I take pride in progress.

June 7:

By encouraging others, I am able to encourage myself.
I do not look down on those who may need motivation.
I know that we all sometimes need to be inspired.
I vow to be strong enough to be a giver of hope,
yet humble enough to receive the light offered by others.

June 8:

Rising with the morning sun is truly a privilege.
I recognize that waking up each morning is not
guaranteed. As I move forward with my day, I will
remember to be grateful for the opportunity to add yet
another page to my legacy.

June 9:

I have the power to decide at any point that this is not
how my story is going to be written. By controlling my
actions, I am the author and editor. Each decision I make
reminds me that I am in control of my life.

June 10:

I possess all of the tools to be the best person I can be.

I am more beautiful than I ever imagined.

June 11:

I am gracious enough to forgive even the undeserving.

I release all of the pain and anger that I have endured at the hands of others.

I am moving forward with my head held high.

I am thankful for the strength I have found because of the suffering I have endured.

June 12:

I vow to be productive, thoughtful, and happy today.

I aim to leave behind remnants of joy with each person whom I encounter. I will shine brightly at every turn.

June 13:

It is important to be intuitive.

I take the time to listen to my mind, body and soul.

I access the things I need to be balanced and healthy.

June 14:

We are all a product of choices. Some were made by us, others were made for us. From this point forward, I am taking lead of my life. Understanding that each choice has an impact, I will carefully choose only the absolute best.

June 15:

I speak the success of the day into existence.
I am calling for the patience, resilience, perseverance and determination needed to be a conqueror.

June 16:

I have the strength, depth, and wisdom to be fulfilling.
Likewise, I possess the open mind, open heart, and humility it takes to be fulfilled.

June 17:

What is meant for me will never be kept from me.
I am at peace knowing that I am exactly where I am supposed to be.

June 18:

I am restored, rejuvenated, and renewed on command.

June 19:

I am strong enough to adapt to life's unforeseen circumstances. However, I can identify when I should not accept unfavorable conditions.

As the author and editor, I am in control of my decisions. I have the power to change how my story is written.

June 20:

I have compassion for others, despite my own circumstances. When necessary, I can encourage myself, so that I am able to uplift others. I understand that being loving, intuitive, selfless and reliable is the biggest gift I can give to those around me.

June 21:

I vow to:

take actions that give me pride,

display character that is influential,

have a heart that is more valuable than gold,

and a soul I am truly in love with.

June 22:

In order to excel, I must first believe in myself.
Though I am far from perfect, I continue to take strides
toward greatness. I have faith in all that I am and all that I
aspire to be.

June 23:

I recognize my full potential. I will live a life I am proud
of with people I am inspired by. I will not settle for
anything less than the absolute best.

June 24:

My ambition does not have a ceiling.
My goals will not be limited.
My determination is endless.

June 25:

I am phenomenal by choice.
My greatness is not accidental.

June 26:

Beauty exists beyond what the eye can see.
I have an obligation to myself to be beautiful in my mind,
heart and sprit.

June 27:
Each day I am a better version of me.
The best has yet to come.

June 28:
I am living in my strength. I have the preparation of the
past to thank for the resilience that exists within me today.

June 29:
I live in the love that radiates from every fiber of my
being. Love flows through me and is received by those in
need. My heart is full and my spirit is luminous. In my
presence, no one will ever feel alone.

June 30:
Every day that I have lived was designed to sculpt the
person that I am. I have seen bright days that kept me
going and dark ones that kept me humble. I am thankful
for both, for I am living a life rich with experiences.

JULY

July 1:
My spirit thrives off of greatness.
I aspire to be exceptional, even at times when it is difficult.

July 2:
I will shine today despite any challenges I may face.
I will allow my inner light to brighten up a room.
My brilliance will not be dulled.

July 3:
Reciprocity is key. I will never ask for something from
another that I am unwilling to deliver myself.

July 4:
Self-reliance is key.
Independence is a gift.
I am capable of being my own lifeline.

July 5:
It is important that I remember to live in the moment.
In order to assure that the greatest times of my life are
cherished, I must remember to pause and be grateful for
the here and now.

July 6:
I will be kind to others knowing that this decision alone
has the power to make someone's day.

July 7:
Without the opportunity to walk a mile in the shoes of
another, it is unfair to judge. I extend the same courtesy to
others that I expect to receive. I will not be judgmental
because I do not want to be judged.

July 8:
I am not defined by how many times I've fallen, but by
how I've gathered my lesson, nursed my wounds and
continued on stronger and wiser.

July 9:
There are certain things that I shall not accept from
others. Likewise, there are things that I would not expect
others to accept from me.

July 10:
I vow to look at the heart of others instead of their faces,
bodies, and style. The reflection of one's spirit is more
important than the external package. I trust that my vision
will be clear and my decisions wise.

July 11:
I am strong enough to let go when necessary and wait for
what I deserve.

July 12:
I will not let things that bring me down dwell in my mind,
in my heart, or in my space.

July 13:
I will offer others the same courtesy, respect, love,
empathy, and grace that I would like to be offered to me.

July 14:
There shall be no complaints about what I have allowed to
happen. If there is something that is not right for me, I
will take action to realign my life's circumstances.

July 15:
I am more than my mistakes, more than my past, and
more than my imperfections.
I am excellent simply because I aspire to be.
That goal alone sets me apart. I accept the responsibility
that comes with being extraordinary.

July 16:

Forgiveness is necessary for progression, forgetting is not. I will forgive the hurt, but I will not forget the truth.

July 17:

I will not allow my wounds to turn me into someone I am not proud to be. I will remain true to the beauty inside of me despite who or what has tried to steal my joy.

July 18:

It is my goal to have a character that is so beautiful; others feel better about themselves just by being in my presence.

July 19:

The presence of individuals with a similar mindset increases my quality of life. My ideal is to have a social circle of people with an elevated sense of self. We will cultivate each other and by spreading our empowerment, increase exponentially.

July 20:

I forgive myself for any mistakes I have made.
I am sure to learn every lesson hidden
in the details of my circumstances.

July 21:
The love that lives within me is gentle enough to be received in abundance, yet strong enough to save a soul.

July 22:
I have the right to pursue happiness and power to ignite fulfillment within.

July 23:
My mind is free of worries;
my conscious free of guilt and my heart is free of hatred.

July 24:
I understand that I am beautifully and perfectly made for the individual that is meant for me.

July 25:
Knowing the difference between right and wrong means I have an obligation. I will make no excuses. I will do what is right, even when it is difficult and inconvenient.

July 26:
I will not allow anyone to tell me what I can and cannot do. There is victory beneath my feet.

July 27:
Even through the toughest times,
I will stand tall and keep my head high.

July 28:
I am unstoppable.
Not because I am flawless,
but because I continue on despite my flaws.

July 29:
I am grateful for who I am today while fighting for who I
want to be tomorrow.

July 30:
There may never be a perfect time or a special sign that
assures me that I am doing the right thing.
I am courageous enough to travel along any path in
pursuit of happiness.

July 31:
My worth never escapes me.
I am completely aware of how invaluable I am.

AUGUST

August 1:
I vow to live beautifully, dream passionately and love completely.

August 2:
Today I will give the world the courtesy of being the very best version of me.

August 3:
I have the faith to venture into the unknown despite self-doubt. I will not be afraid to take the next step.

August 4:
I surround myself with people that lift me higher.

August 5:
I will socialize in kindness, with grace and with love. I'll stand with others in time of need. I will not turn my back on those that rely on me.

August 6:
It is my divine right to protect my peace.
Anything or anyone that is not conducive to this effort shall be dismissed.

August 7:

My emotional, mental, physical and spiritual health is my first priority. I understand that if I am not at my best, I am unable to be there for those that may need me.

Though I am a selfless individual, it is important at times to put myself first.

August 8:

I remember to be grateful for all of the many things that are going well in my life.

August 9:

It is always a good time to be courageous.

August 10:

Happiness today is not optional, it is mandatory. I vow that as I go through the day, my thoughts and actions will be a reflection of this decision.

August 11:

Patience is a virtue.

I am satisfied knowing that I have lived some of my best days, and still have better ones ahead.

August 12:

I will not be limited by the standards, perceptions, and opinions of others.

August 13:

Each day I give my very best to the people in my life and the tasks at hand. I have an obligation to put my best foot forward. I therefore have the right to receive the very best this world has to offer. I will not settle!

August 14:

To be a follower is effortless. To be a leader means to be brave, strong and not easily swayed or influenced by the masses. I have all of the traits necessary to stand out from the crowd and lead those aspiring to greatness.

August 15:

I have an abundance of talent.
My opportunities are endless.

August 16:

There is beauty in waking up each day. Despite what is happening in my life, I will never forget to be grateful for the chance to continue living my legacy.

August 17:
I attract love and meaningful relationships.

August 18:
Love and compassion radiate from me.

August 19:
I am constantly evolving.
I am humble and grateful for this truth.

August 20:
I vow to create my own sunshine
at times where there is none.

August 21:
I am one of a kind.

August 22:
Though I've stared in the face of rejection, I will always be
good enough for what and who is meant for me.

August 23:
Forgiveness is essential to healing.
I am interested only in a healthy healing process.

August 24:

By aggressively pursuing excellence

I am likely to prosper abundantly.

August 25:

I will not settle for less than I deserve.

August 26:

Excellence requires effort.

I have exactly what it takes to be phenomenal!

August 27:

The happiness of those I love is of utmost importance to me.

August 28:

There have been times when I doubted myself and have forgotten my worth.

Those times are in the past. My future consists of unbreakable strength and restored dignity.

August 29:
Time will heal wounds.
I have survived the past.
As a stronger and wiser individual,
I will surely survive present day.

August 30:
There is pride and satisfaction in doing what is right.
I take the time to evaluate my choices in order to make the best one each and every time.

August 31:
It is not uncommon to want what you can't have.
It is however; degrading to chase what does not want to be caught. I will be wise enough to know when to move on.

SEPTEMBER

September 1:
I am delightful!

September 2:
The fire within me can't be extinguished.

September 3:
I am beautiful, I am strong and I am talented, but most importantly, I am humble.

September 4:
There is nothing or no one that can stop a star from twinkling. I have a light that shall not be dimmed!

September 5:
I have decided that I will be excellent.
I will pursue greatness at every turn.

September 6:
I am worthy of every blessing I have received and those that are coming my way.

September 7:
I treat people how I would like to be treated. Not only in their presence, but when they are not around as well.

September 8:

I will not dwell in the past.

Everything that happened in my life has its place and purpose. I can only learn and move on.

September 9:

Every day will present a new challenge. I channel renewed strength and determination to face what lies ahead.

September 10:

People can bring out the best in you. They can also bring out the worst in you if you allow them to. I will take control of my actions and behavior despite provocation.

September 11:

I find comfort in knowing that I have people that care about my well being. I appreciate my loved ones this day and every day.

September 12:

Approaching any goal with 100% dedication and determination is something I can be proud of.

September 13:
I am an intelligent person with all of the resources I need to make the best decision possible at all times.

September 14:
I have a strong determination to be successful.
I will not lose!

September 15:
Standing up for what I believe in is not an option,
but a requirement.

September 16:
I am genuine.

September 17:
Mistakes sometimes need to be made in order for lessons to be learned. I am open to trial and error in pursuit of my personal triumph.

September 18:
The relationships I cherish most are ones that are healthy and with people who love me unconditionally.

September 19:
Kindness toward others is important to me. I offer those around me all that I want in return.

September 20:
The best things about me can never be compromised.

September 21:
I am insightful.

September 22:
There is no ceiling in regard to what I am able to achieve. My dreams are sky high and so is my will power!

September 23:
Putting forth effort to build up another person is fulfilling. Allowing their energy to be restored from mine is an honor.

September 24:
Though I will not relate to every person I meet, I will try my very best to be patient with good spirited individuals despite any differences we may have.

September 25:
I've been given the gift of greatness.

September 26:
It is wise to be selective of who is allowed into my heart and protective over those individuals once they are there.

September 27:
I am compassionate.

September 28:
Validation from others is not something that I will ever need to understand my worth.

September 29:
Appreciation is extended for all of the beautiful things I have had the pleasure to experience in my lifetime.

September 30:
It is imperative to be open to constructive criticism.
I understand that I am not perfect.
There is always room for improvement.

OCTOBER

October 1:
I am powerful

October 2:
My happiness will not be
diluted by the opinions of others.

October 3:
The relationships I cherish will not be compromised by
distance. I will not allow physical location to dictate the
bond I have with close friends and family.

October 4:
At times people will not understand, relate or agree with
me. This does not mean that I am on the wrong path. I
will stay on course in pursuit of my divine destiny.

October 5:
Signs from the universe will present themselves in certain
situations. I will be wise enough to recognize them and
strong enough to accept them even if they aren't what I
hoped for.

October 6:
Giving people the benefit of the doubt is important to me. I will not automatically think negatively about a person. I will allow them room to show me who they are.

October 7:
I am mindful that the decisions I make today will be the reality I live tomorrow.

October 8:
I am in love with life.

October 9:
I am powerful.

October 10:
I never wish misfortune on others. Even when someone has something that I want, I am not envious. I know that being truly happy for others releases an energy that will be returned ten-fold.

October 11:
I will refrain from behavior that does not reflect who I truly am and my fundamental beliefs.

October 12:
I am at peace within.

October 13:
I will continue to be more than what is popular amongst the masses. I am not afraid to go my own way.

October 14:
Growth is sometimes uncomfortable, as it may require venturing into the unknown. I will refuse to remain stagnant and hidden away in my comfort zone.

October 15:
I understand that in some situations I have to create my own closure. I will move on with words unspoken because I refuse to remain broken.

October 16:
People can count on me during times of need.
I am able to separate from the burden of others from that of my own. I will not be weighed down by what is not mine to carry.

October 17:

Actions are more powerful than intentions.

Each day I strive to do all that I intend to do in order to show the world the loving, nurturing, progressive talent that lives within.

October 18:

Helping others comes naturally to me. I can be strong for others when they are temporarily weak. I can be a source of energy for the souls that need to be refueled.

October 19:

I am impactful.

October 20:

Every blessing assigned to me is on the way.

October 21:

Investing in myself is mandatory. I will take the time and make every effort to be at my best physically, mentally, emotionally, and spiritually.

October 22:

Success cannot be achieved where there is no dedication and discipline.

October 23:
Wanting the best in life means
I must not be willing to settle for less.

October 24:
Talent is meaningless if it is not applied and appreciated
by the individual to whom it was given. I put forth every
effort to display my talent and recognize that it is a gift.

October 25:
I am capable of achieving all of my goals.

October 26:
When difficult times present themselves,
I channel strength that lives deep within.
I've been through many things. I am equipped with tools I
need to heal and move forward.

October 27:
Art makes the world an interesting place to live in.
I appreciate the many different art forms and respect
artists of all kinds.

October 28:

How people handle themselves under pressure speaks to their character. I will not compromise my morals as a result of increased stress levels.

October 29:

Perfection can never be attained. I can however, achieve excellence and plan to pursue it each day of my life.

October 30:

I have an abundance of love.

October 31:

Without believing in my own qualities, I am unable to inspire others. I consistently reassure myself of my own value so that I can always be a positive influence.

NOVEMBER

November 1:
I am insightful.

November 2:
I am advancing continuously.
I will not allow anything to stunt my growth.

November 3:
Love conquers all.
It cancels out fear and overpowers hate.
My love for others is my greatest achievement.

November 4:
Each day I am a little closer to my goals.

November 5:
I am loyal.

November 6:
My expertise makes me invaluable.
My skills are constantly developing.

November 7:

I cherish each meaningful relationship that has developed throughout my lifetime. I wish the very best for not only those in my life, but also for those that are no longer a part of it.

November 8:

I am an honest person.

I stand by my word.

November 9:

What is truly mine can never be kept from me.

Knowing this brings me peace and comfort.

November 10:

I am not interested in conformity.

November 11:

I am strong willed!

November 12:

There are incredible things in the works for me.

I am ready to receive all the universe has to offer.

November 13:
The person I am today is someone I will be proud of
years from now. If I find myself doing or being something
that makes me feel otherwise, I am honest with myself
and able to adjust.

November 14:
Today I will focus on the celebration of life.
I will make no complaints about what does not matter in
the grand scheme of things.
I look to the future with gratitude and hope.

November 15:
I vow to keep myself open to happiness.

November 16:
I am soft hearted and good-natured.

November 17:
Growth means that some former behavior, activities and/
or reactions are no longer suitable. I know that I must be
open to change in order to advance.

November 18:
I channel the light that is required to drive out darkness
and the love required to drive out hate.

November 19:
Negativity takes different shapes, wears many masks, and comes in several forms. I am wise enough to recognize it and strong enough to stand against it at all times.

November 20:
The best days of my life are ahead of me!

November 21:
I will disprove anyone that doubts my abilities.
This includes the voice within that sometimes tells me to run from the unknown.

November 22:
I will not allow negative thoughts to linger. I beckon a frame of mind conducive to healing and progression.

November 23:
I strive to see the beauty in every person; especially in those who have forgotten to see beauty in themselves.

November 24:
It is mandatory that I believe in myself!

November 25:
Access to my happiness will not be granted to others.

November 26:
Love is not something that should be forced. I deserve
love that is pure, effortless, and unconditional.

November 27:
As human beings, we seek closure in order to heal.
I understand that sometimes closure never comes.
I have the strength to move on without it.

November 28:
Though I have seen dark days and been hurt by
individuals, I am able to appreciate the good in
the world and the beauty in people.

November 29:
I am deserving of the break-through coming my way.

November 30:
There is beauty in courage.
There is inspiration in the ability to be bold.

DECEMBER

December 1:
I am extraordinary!

December 2:
I am loving and kind.

December 3:
I am genius in my own right.

December 4:
I am patient with myself and with others.

December 5:
I am humble.

December 6:
I am a person who chooses wisely.

December 7:
I am a gentle, loving, and incredible individual with much
to offer the world.

December 8:
I am a perfect product of both my good and bad times.

December 9:
I am destined for greatness.

December 10:
I am unique.

December 11:
I am willing to admit when I am wrong.

December 12:
I am graceful.

December 13:
I am capable of forgiveness.

December 14:
I am walking in excellence.

December 15:
I am goal oriented.

December 16:
I am a survivor!

December 17:
I am beautiful.

December 18:
I am loved.

December 19:
I am strong.

December 20:
I am resilient.

December 21:
I am determined.

December 22:
I am unstoppable.

December 23:
I am passionate.

December 24:
I am authentic.

December 25:

Love, joy, peace and gratitude are my focus today.

I am thankful for all of my blessings.

Despite the hard times that I have seen, I know there are many who are not as fortunate as I am.

I will not make any complaints on this day.

Instead, I hope for nourishment, warmth, and love for all of those in need.

December 26:

I am full of life and joy.

December 27:

I am prosperous.

December 28:

I am invaluable.

December 29:

I am honorable.

December 30:

I am receptive to all of the happiness, and great energy the universe has to offer me.

December 31:

I have a vision, I've set my goals.

I will surround myself with people that are conducive to my evolution. I will be unapologetic as I transition, even if I have to leave certain people and things behind.

My time as a caterpillar is up. My wings are ready!

KIA WOODS was born in New York City, where she had to grow up very quickly. Through unfavorable living conditions and hardships faced in her early years, the author was determined to be a role model to her two younger sisters, Tas and Ashley. Very early on, Kia felt that success could be achieved via education. She began reading short novels at the age of 4, where she would escape temporarily  into the lives of the characters. At age 12, she began to compete in poetry contests after being inspired by her older sister Orissa. In 2004, she earned a place on the *Youth Speaks NY* team and had the opportunity to compete on a National level in LA. As a result of that accomplishment, Kia is one of the youngest poets to have performed at *Nuyorican Poets Cafe* in NYC. As she builds her corporate career, Kia continues to write on relatable subjects. Poetry is her first love and Kia feels her calling is to use her gift to inspire a mindset adjustment while encouraging and engaging her audience. She hopes one day, to make motivational speaking appearances on a full time basis.

Kia comes from a large family, and her other beloved sisters and brothers are: Alasha, Corrine, Kristen, Joey, Maurice and the late Lavar.

NOTES

Made in the USA
Las Vegas, NV
02 January 2022

40106636R00083